BE A MASON

Published in the United States of America by Cherry Lake Publishing
Ann Arbor, Michigan
www.cherrylakepublishing.com

Content Adviser: Robert Arnold, National Director of Apprenticeship, Training and Education, International Masonry Training and Education Foundation
Reading Adviser: Marla Conn, MS, Ed., Literacy specialist, Read-Ability, Inc.

Photo Credits: Cover and pages 1, 12, and 19, ©goodluz/Shutterstock; page 5, ©Dmitry Kalinovsky/Shutterstock; page 6, ©Diego Cervo/Shutterstock; pages 8 and 22, courtesy of the International Masonry Training and Education Foundation; page 11, ©Rido/Shutterstock; page 14, ©JP WALLET/Shutterstock; page 16, ©Monkey Business Images/Shutterstock; page 20, ©TAKAZAWA/Shutterstock; page 25, ©Cineberg/Shutterstock; page 26, ©ALPA PROD/Shutterstock; page 28, ©Phat1978/Shutterstock

Library of Congress Cataloging-in-Publication Data
Names: Mara, Wil, author.
Title: Be a mason / by Wil Mara.
Description: Ann Arbor, Michigan : Cherry Lake Publishing, [2019] | Series: 21st century skills library | Includes bibliographical references and index.
Identifiers: LCCN 2019003503| ISBN 9781534148239 (lib. bdg.) | ISBN 9781534149663 (pdf) | ISBN 9781534151093 (pbk.) | ISBN 9781534152526 (ebook)
Subjects: LCSH: Masonry—Vocational guidance—Juvenile literature.
Classification: LCC TH5325 .M37 2019 | DDC 693/.1023—dc23
LC record available at https://lccn.loc.gov/2019003503

Cherry Lake Publishing would like to acknowledge the work of The Partnership for 21st Century Learning. Please visit www.p21.org for more information.

Printed in the United States of America
Corporate Graphics

ABOUT THE AUTHOR

Wil Mara is the author of over 175 fiction and nonfiction books for children. He has written many titles for Cherry Lake Publishing, including the popular *Global Citizens: Modern Media* and *Citizen's Guide* series. More about his work can be found at www.wilmara.com.

TABLE OF CONTENTS

CHAPTER 1

The Mason's Life

Steve Lopez gets up at 6:30 a.m. sharp, just like he does every day. It doesn't take him long to get ready and eat a good breakfast, so he's out the door not long after waking up. The magnetic sign on the side of his truck reads "Stephen J. Lopez, Master Mason." Steve has been involved in masonry for almost all of his adult life. A mason is someone who builds things out of brick, block, and stone. There are many different kinds of work within the masonry field, and Steve has done all of it. He loves this variety because it keeps things interesting. Each day brings a different challenge. And he's always learning. The more experience he gets, the better

If you've ever seen a brick building, you've seen the work of a mason.

he becomes at his job. Thinking about some of his most impressive and creative work makes Steve smile. He could never handle the kind of job where you're doing the same thing all the time.

Steve has to travel about a half hour to today's job **site**. He's been at this site for the last two months, and the project is just about finished. A new house is going up, and it's a big one. The owner is a wealthy businessman, and he wanted a lot of custom

Members of a construction crew often meet at the beginning of the day to discuss what needs to be done.

stonework on the property. For the first two weeks, Steve cut and laid down stones called pavers for the patio around the pool. He also had to put together a fountain with a fish sculpture that had water coming out its mouth. After that, Steve helped to lay the house's **foundation**. Then he and some other masons laid each stone in the driveway. Now that the rest of the house has been built, Steve has been working on the outside steps. There are two sets—one in the front and one in the back.

Steve arrives at the site around 8:00. Most of the other workers are there, too. Carpenters, plumbers, electricians, and many others are all preparing to start the day's work. Steve has been working with these people every day since the project started, and he has gotten to know some of them very well. He really likes this aspect of his job. After years of working at different sites, he has made many friends in the construction business. He stops and chats with a few of them before going to see the **foreman**. The two of them discuss the day's schedule and decide that Steve should finish up the front steps before starting on the ones out back. Furniture movers, painters, and carpet layers will all be coming within the next few days, and they'll need to get into the house through the front door.

Steve gets his tools out of the truck and brings them to the front of the house. Among them are drills and saws made especially for masonry work. Some of the drill bits and saw blades have pieces of real diamonds on their tips. That's because diamonds are among the hardest substances in the world. They can even cut through solid stone!

Mortar is a wet paste that hardens as it dries. Masons use a tool called a trowel to spread it and form clean edges.

A **pallet** of building stones is waiting for him. He mixes his **mortar** in a shallow tub and gets to work. He has to lay the stones into place one at a time. He makes sure each one is lined up perfectly with the others before moving on to the next one. He also makes sure the mortar looks neat and clean by scraping off any excess before it has a chance to harden. After working all morning, Steve takes an hour-long break for lunch and hangs out with his friends while they eat. Then it's back to the job. All the stones are in place by the end of the day. Tomorrow the mortar will be fully hardened, and then the steps can be used.

As Steve drives back home, he thinks about how those steps will probably be there for decades to come. Hundreds of people will use them, going in and out of the house, and lots of memories will be made on them. And he was the one who built them. He always thinks about this when he finishes a project. Knowing that his work will stand the test of time is one of the most rewarding parts of his career.

21st Century Content

There are about 300,000 masonry workers employed in the United States. Among the most common are brick and block layers. The states that employ the most are listed below, along with the most current estimated employment figures:

- New York: 6,300
- Florida: 4,400
- California: 3,900
- Texas: 3,900
- Pennsylvania: 3,300

CHAPTER 2

Becoming a Mason

Masons are in high demand in the construction industry. There are not enough qualified workers to fill all of the masonry-related jobs available today. This means masonry is a good career choice if you are interested in the building trades. Not just anyone can start laying bricks and stones and expect to do a good job, though. Becoming a mason requires specialized knowledge and training.

High school classes provide the general information that will become the backbone of a mason's career knowledge. For example, math is an everyday part of masonry work. Algebra and geometry skills are especially helpful. A mason

Anyone who wants to become a mason would
do well to pay close attention in math class.

During an apprenticeship, a masonry student can learn the details of the trade from someone with years or even decades of experience.

uses this knowledge to take measurements and cut pieces of stone to the correct size and shape. Math also helps masons determine the quantities of different materials they will need for a job.

Most masons do not attend college after high school. Some of them choose to attend a technical school. Here, they will start learning the basics of masonry and construction in general through classroom education. Classes cover everything from the basics of bricklaying and how to read masonry **blueprints** to the specific uses of different tools and building materials. Students might also study math subjects relating directly to masonry, such as cost estimation.

Even if aspiring masons attend technical school, they will still need to complete an **apprenticeship** before starting work as professional masons. During an apprenticeship, the student, or apprentice, works on real job sites under the supervision of an experienced mason. This allows the apprentice to get plenty of real hands-on experience without the risk of making major mistakes.

Masons use wood forms to shape concrete or show where stones should go. When the project is done, they remove the wood forms.

Masonry apprentices learn every step of the process. They will help plan and design structures and choose the appropriate materials for projects. They will learn to clear and prepare a work area at the start of a new project. This might include laying down wooden patterns or forms to show how bricks or stones will be arranged and aligned. They will develop their skills at placing stones and mortar neatly and efficiently.

As an apprentice works, their **mentor** watches, giving instruction where necessary and answering whatever questions the apprentice may have. As the apprentice becomes more skilled, the mentor doesn't need to provide as much supervision. By the end of the apprenticeship, the student will likely be able to complete most jobs without any assistance at all. A masonry apprenticeship can last anywhere from three to four years, so the apprentice and the mentor often form a close bond.

After the apprenticeship is over, a student mason is required to take tests in order to earn their final certification. These tests will demonstrate both classroom knowledge and hands-on skills. The testing varies slightly from state to state, but the main points are the same.

Apprentices who successfully complete this testing are legally able to work on their own. At this point, the apprentice becomes a journeyworker. Becoming a master mason comes later on, after a journeyworker mason builds up more professional experience and further education.

A stonemason might do custom carving work for customers.

Life and Career Skills

There are several different professions within the masonry field. Some masons specialize in just one area, while others take on many different types of jobs.

- Brickmasons and blockmasons specialize in laying traditional bricks and other stone blocks to build foundations, steps, walls, walkways, and other structures.
- Cement masons and finishers use concrete to form sidewalks, garage floors, and other surfaces.
- Stonemasons often work with natural-cut stone like marble or granite to produce beautiful finished work such as kitchen countertops.
- Terrazzo masons put together decorative stone walkways, patios, and panels.

The first two professions have more practical value, while the other two are more artistic. But all require great patience and attention to detail.

On the Job

The daily working life of a mason presents both challenges and terrific rewards. On average, a mason can expect to earn about $43,000 per year. That salary, of course, will increase with a mason's experience. Those who work in especially difficult areas of the masonry trade have a chance to earn more than average. Master masons earn the highest salaries and are the most in demand.

Becoming a truly great mason requires a certain type of personality. For example, masons should enjoy working outside. While they might move indoors from time to time to complete a job, almost all of their work will take place outdoors. Jobs such as building steps, laying a driveway,

Working as a mason requires physical strength.

Getting the chance to work outside on a nice day is one of the top perks of being a mason.

rebuilding a crumbling wall, or assembling a fountain all require a mason to work out in the elements. This means working as a mason is ideal for someone who can't stand the idea of being in an office all day. But while working in the fresh air and sunshine might sound wonderful, there will also be days when the weather isn't quite so pleasant. Unless conditions are so awful that work is called off altogether, a mason may sometimes have to work in the frigid cold, blistering heat, snow, rain, and high wind.

21st Century Content

The masonry industry is growing at a faster rate than most others. The number of available jobs increases by about 12 percent per year. Overall, there are about 300,000 masonry jobs in the United States, and experts expect that number to rise by about another 34,000 over the next 10 years.

The majority of masonry workers are cement masons and finishers. These workers represent about 61 percent of the field. Brickmasons and blockmasons are next, at 31 percent. Stonemasons make up about 6 percent of the workforce. Terrazzo workers are the smallest group in the profession, at roughly 1 percent.

Masons frequently check to make sure their work is perfectly level. If just one or two bricks are uneven, it can affect everything that gets stacked on top of them.

Being a mason also requires a great deal of patience. Working with stone is not something that can be done quickly. Measurements and other planning need to be exact. Stones have to be cut precisely, and assembling them can only be accomplished one piece at a time. Each one must be carefully aligned as it is set in place. This helps masons make sure their work is both **level** and **plumb**. Custom stonework—such as creating statues from scratch or shaping pavers to build a unique walkway—can take hours, days, or even weeks to produce. But for the type of person who doesn't mind taking their time, such work can be very satisfying.

It is extremely important for masons to maintain good physical health. Working with heavy materials such as brick and stone can put strain on the body. Only those who keep themselves in excellent physical shape will be able to withstand such activity over the long haul. There are a number of special devices designed to help masons lift and place stonework of all sizes. These range from hoists and pulleys to motor-driven cranes. But even with such helpful tools at their disposal, there will be times when masons need to do some heavy lifting on their own.

A mason also has to be comfortable working both alone and as part of a team. A construction site usually has many people performing many different tasks. And because most construction projects can last anywhere from a few weeks to a year or more, the construction team needs to get along. Masons may work on their specific duties by themselves, but chances are high that they'll be working around at least a few other people.

CHAPTER 4

Rules and Regulations

Being a mason isn't always just about working with bricks and stones. Masons who run their own contracting businesses also have to deal with legal and business aspects of the profession.

Contracts are a big part of many construction careers. A contract is a written agreement to perform a job in exchange for payment. Just about every masonry job will be arranged with a written agreement before the work actually starts. A contract serves to outline what each side expects from the other, and what each side will receive as a result of the arrangement. It could include such details as a deadline for the work to be completed and a schedule of when the worker will be paid.

Masons and other trade workers should always make sure they understand the details of a project before agreeing to work on it.

Experienced masons know to carefully pay attention to the language used in a contract. This helps them avoid getting caught in bad situations. For example, what happens if a mason gets sick and is unable to complete a job by the agreed-upon date? Do they still get paid during that sick time? What if there's an accident on the job through no fault of their own, but they become injured and can't work? Will the employer continue to pay them and also cover their medical expenses? These types of issues should be decided well in advance.

A license helps a mason show customers that they are skilled and knowledgeable in their trade.

A mason contractor also needs a **license**. Getting a license allows mason contractors to prove that they are reliable professionals. A mason's license is usually issued through the state in which they work. (If a mason has to work in another state, they may need to check and see if they will be covered

Life and Career Skills

Safety on the job site is essential for masons and other construction workers. There are heavy materials being moved around all the time. Many of the tools needed to complete jobs can also be dangerous. This means masons need to be careful at all times, both to keep themselves safe and to protect fellow workers from harm. Many states have legal regulations in place to make construction work safer. Individual companies and job sites might have their own safety policies to follow as well.

A variety of safety gear can also help protect masons as they work. Gloves and body braces can help masons avoid injury while lifting heavy stones. Hard hats and reinforced boots keep them safe from falling objects. Breathing filters called respirators are important when cutting stones, because the dust produced while making cuts is bad for the lungs.

A career in masonry offers the chance to create amazing things.

under the license from their home state.) Most states require masons to pass a test to earn their license. Others offer it upon completion of an apprenticeship, with no further testing required.

Some masons work without getting licensed, but this is risky and illegal. Punishments can range from costly fines to being prevented from applying for a license for a period of time. Employers who hire unlicensed masons are also breaking the law. Furthermore, most unlicensed masons fail to obtain a license because they lack the necessary skills or experience. A licensed mason can be trusted to get work done in a timely and professional manner.

Being **bonded** is another important legal requirement for mason contractors. A bond is a type of insurance policy. It covers all sorts of mishaps that could happen on the job. If a mason gets hurt while working, the bond will cover at least some of the medical costs. A bond also covers the costs of any mistakes a mason might make while working. No matter how much experience a professional tradesperson has, they're still human and prone to error. For example, a mason might put up a brick wall. If some flaw in the structure causes it to come crashing down, the bricks could then land on construction equipment or a vehicle parked nearby. All the damage caused by this—which would likely be quite expensive—would be covered by the mason's bond. And though bond insurance is extremely important to have, it's even better to never have a reason to use it!

Think About It

People have been practicing masonry in one form or another for literally thousands of years. In fact, stonemasonry is considered one of the oldest trades in human history. Throughout time, masons were usually regarded as true artisans and respected by the rest of their society. How do you suppose early stoneworkers carved natural stones into pleasing and suitable shapes? How do you think they moved them without the aid of cranes and other modern devices? What bonding material do you think they used to hold simple bricks and other stones together?

If you were going to become a mason, which specialty would interest you the most? Which would interest you the least? Think it through carefully and explain your answer.

Find Out More

BOOKS

Capici, Gaetano. *What Does It Do? Cement Mixer*. Ann Arbor, MI: Cherry Lake Publishing, 2011.

Duke, Shirley. *Pyramids of Egypt*. Vero Beach, FL: Rourke Educational Media, 2015.

Rhatigan, Joe. *Get a Job at a Construction Site*. Ann Arbor, MI: Cherry Lake Publishing, 2017.

WEBSITES

BBC—History: The Medieval Stonemason
www.bbc.co.uk/history/british/middle_ages/architecture_medmason_01.shtml
Find out how stonemasons constructed incredible buildings in Great Britain hundreds of years ago.

U.S. Bureau of Labor Statistics—Occupational Outlook Handbook: Masonry Workers
https://www.bls.gov/ooh/construction-and-extraction/brickmasons-blockmasons-and-stonemasons.htm
Learn how to become a mason and find out more about the profession at this government site.

GLOSSARY

apprenticeship (uh-PREN-tis-ship) training situation in which someone learns a skill by working with an expert on the job

blueprints (BLOO-printz) drawings that illustrate how a structure needs to be built

bonded (BAHND-id) having an insurance policy to cover damages caused by a worker while on the job

foreman (FOR-muhn) the person in charge of a construction job

foundation (foun-DAY-shuhn) the lowest level of a structure, upon which the rest of the structure is built

level (LEV-uhl) having a flat, even, horizontal surface

license (LYE-suhns) an official certification that someone is qualified to perform a job

mentor (MEN-tor) someone who teaches a less experienced person

mortar (MOR-tur) bonding material designed to hold stones together after it dries

pallet (PA-lit) a platform upon which large quantities of individual stones can be delivered

plumb (PLUHM) perfectly straight up and down

site (SITE) the location of a masonry job

INDEX